LOST LIBERTIES

THE WAR MEASURES ACT

Xavier Gélinas and Mélanie Morin-Pelletier

CANADIAN MUSEUM OF HISTORY
MUSÉE CANADIEN DE L'HISTOIRE

Library and Archives Canada
Cataloguing in Publication

Title: Lost Liberties: The War Measures Act / Xavier Gélinas and Mélanie Morin-Pelletier.

Names: Gélinas, Xavier, 1967- author. | Morin-Pelletier, Mélanie, 1980- author | Canadian Museum of History, issuing body.

Series: Souvenir catalogue series ; 28.

Description: Series statement: Souvenir catalogue series, ISSN 2291-6385; 28 | Issued also in French under title: Libertés sacrifiées.

Identifiers: Canadiana 20210297530 | ISBN 9780660343679 (softcover)

Subjects: LCSH: Canada. War Measures Act. | LCSH: Canadian Museum of History—Catalogs. | LCSH: War and emergency legislation—Canada—History—20th century. | LCSH: War and emergency powers—Canada—History—20th century. | LCSH: Civil rights—Political aspects—Canada. | LCSH: Minorities—Canada—Social conditions—20th century. | LCSH: Canada—Politics and government—20th century. | LCGFT: Catalogs.

Classification: LCC JC599.C3 G45 2021 | DDC 323.09710904—dc23

Published by the Canadian Museum of History
100 Laurier Street
Gatineau, QC K1A 0M8
historymuseum.ca

Printed and bound in Canada

Graphic design by: Maestro

This work is a souvenir of a special exhibition developed by the Canadian Museum of History, and generously supported by a grant from the Endowment Council of the Canadian First World War Internment Recognition Fund.

Cover image: Glenbow Archives, NC-54-4336

Contents

FOREWORD

Democracies are works in progress.

They are, surely, the form of social organization most likely to achieve great things, both over time and in the hothouse of domestic or international crisis.

But they have also proven catastrophically vulnerable.

Domestic fears, real and imagined, have all too often mutated into punitive efforts at cultural domination. Majorities have tyrannized minorities. Affluence and interest have combined to undermine equality and opportunity. Representative institutions have stifled or resisted social reform or inclusiveness in the name of country or status quo, equating — loudly — dissent with disloyalty.

The exhibition upon which this catalogue is based explores three Canadian invocations of the federal *War Measures Act*, during three periods of national crisis. Two are world wars, and the third a domestic crisis that appeared to represent something tantamount to insurrection.

In each instance, democratic leaders, acting under conditions of uncertainty, risk and intense public pressure, moved reflexively, perhaps even instinctually, toward self-preservation. The tools of state power invigilated, objectified and incarcerated. In each, sectional or racial protagonists draped their platforms in the bunting of nation, state and cause. In each, crisis bred arbitrariness. And in each, blunt actions, undertaken ostensibly in defence of liberty, in fact put it entirely at risk.

The **Lost Liberties** exhibition and catalogue remind us that democracies are not just defined by the casting of ballots and the peaceful transitions of governments. They are defined equally by their actions under conditions of extreme duress, when most deeply threatened, or most vocally decried. Courage is easy in the absence of cost, while principles and values demand more than rhetorical adherence.

I am honoured to have played a small part in the production of this exhibition and catalogue, alongside so many generous partners, talented colleagues and brilliant advisers. It is one of the most important and timely that the Canadian Museum of History has ever produced.

Dean F. Oliver
Senior Director, Research and Chief Curator
Canadian Museum of History

INTRODUCTION

In Western countries, civil liberties date back to the *Magna Carta* of 1215. They include, for example, freedom of expression, freedom of peaceful assembly, the presumption of innocence and the right to a fair, impartial and speedy trial.

In times of crisis, these freedoms can become precarious. Should they be limited to maintain the security of State and society?

During the 20th century, Canada has restricted rights and freedoms a number of times — sometimes for decades. This souvenir catalogue for the exhibition **Lost Liberties** explores three crises in Canadian history that resulted in the suspension of civil liberties. For each — the First World War, the Second World War, and the 1970 October Crisis — the federal government invoked the *War Measures Act*, restricting the freedoms of thousands of individuals.

Each of these three periods is explored in two ways. First, we look at the decision-makers. Who were they? How did they view the national crisis? Next, you will encounter individuals and families affected by these events. What did they experience? How did they express themselves?

We have done our best to let people speak for themselves, from a variety of perspectives. As a result, it is primarily through quotations, photographs, drawings and objects that this difficult aspect of our history is examined.

Italian-Canadian Internee

By Vincenzo Poggi
1940

> **▌▌** No free man shall be seized or imprisoned, or stripped of his rights or possessions, or outlawed or exiled, […] except by the lawful judgment of his equals or by the law of the land. **▌▌**
>
> ***Magna Carta***
> 1215

01

The First World War:
Liberty Shattered

A Country in Turmoil

From 1914 to 1918, Canada was engaged in the bloodiest conflict in its history. The country's entry into the war was marked by patriotic fervour and disorder, a feeling of urgency, and the government's determination to use every means at its disposal to calm public fears.

By virtue of the *War Measures Act* of August 1914, the federal government began to do a number of things which it would never have dreamed of doing in time of peace.

Donald Creighton
Historian

Wartime Recruitment Poster

1914–1918

WE WILL UPHOLD THE PRICELESS GEM OF LIBERTY

" *For Gold the Merchant Ploughs the Main*
The Farmer tills the Manor
But Glory is the Soldier's Prize
The Soldier's Wealth is Honour "

SHALL WE HELP TO CRUSH TYRANNY?

APPLY AT RECRUITING STATION

Canada at War

As a Dominion within the British Empire, Canada was automatically at war when Great Britain declared war on Germany.

During the state of emergency that ensued, the Canadian government adopted unprecedented measures to mobilize for the war effort, uphold national security, and maintain social order.

// We stand shoulder to shoulder with Britain and the other British dominions in this quarrel [...] to uphold principles of liberty, to withstand forces that would convert the world into an armed camp. //

Robert Borden
Prime Minister of Canada
August 19, 1914

Robert Borden (centre)

1915

The *War Measures Act*, August 22, 1914

Hastily drawn up and unanimously adopted by Parliament, the *War Measures Act* gave the federal government sweeping powers to conduct the war, while ensuring the "security, defence, peace, order and welfare of Canada." The law allowed the suspension of civil liberties in the name of national security, and remained in effect until January 1920.

> **//** Make absolutely sure that you omit no power that the government may need. **//**
>
> **Edward Macdonald**
>
> Liberal M.P., speaking to lawyer W. F. O'Connor, who drafted the *War Measures Act* August 1914

▶

First page of *An Act to confer certain powers upon the Governor in Council and to amend the Immigration Act*

1914

Chap. 2.

An Act to confer certain powers upon the Governor in Council and to amend the Immigration Act.

Assented to Saturday, August 22nd 1914

HIS Majesty by and with the advice and consent of the Senate and House of Commons of Canada, enacts as follows:—

1. This Act may be cited as *The War Measures Act, 1914.* Short title.

2. All acts and things done or omitted to be done prior to the passing of this Act and on or after the first day of August, A.D. 1914, by or under the authority of or ratified by,— Ratification of acts already done

(a) His Majesty the King in Council;

(b) Any Minister or officer of His Majesty's Imperial Government;

(c) The Governor in Council;

(d) Any Minister or officer of the Government of Canada;

(e) Any other authority or person;

which, had they been done or omitted after the passing of this Act, would have been authorized by this Act or by orders or regulations hereunder, shall be deemed to have been done or omitted under the authority of this Act and are hereby declared to have been lawfully done or omitted.

3. The provisions of sections 6, 10, 11 and 13 of this Act shall only be in force during war, invasion, or insurrection, real or apprehended. Limiting sections 6, 10, 11 and 13

4. The issue of a proclamation by His Majesty, or under the authority of the Governor in Council shall be conclusive evidence that war, invasion, or insurrection, real or apprehended, exists and has existed for any period of time therein stated and of its continuance, until by the issue of a further proclamation it is declared that the war invasion or insurrection no longer exists. Evidence of war etc.

2—1

National Security First

The decisions made by Canadian courts during the war generally reflected the importance of national security, to the detriment of individual rights, including freedom from arbitrary arrest and detention.

Although staunch defenders of civil liberties in times of peace, judges rarely opposed repressive measures adopted by the federal government in wartime.

> It must be the general safety first in all things always; until the final victory is won; even though individuals may suffer meanwhile.
>
> **Richard Martin Meredith**
> Chief Justice of the Ontario Court of Common Pleas
> January 1915

Toronto Daily News
October 24, 1914

Alien Enemies Have No Rights in Court

Even Action Begun Before War Cannot be Gone on With

An interesting alien enemy case was aired yesterday before Chief Justice Falconbridge at Osgoode Hall. A motion for a stay of proceedings on behalf of his Austrian clients, Feko Dumenco and his wife,

Public Hostility Toward "Enemy Aliens"

Actively encouraged by the Canadian government, hundreds of thousands of immigrants from Germany and the Austro-Hungarian Empire had settled in Canada by the turn of the 20th century. The discrimination they had already suffered was greatly heightened in wartime.

In the mines of British Columbia and Nova Scotia, workers went on strike to demand that immigrants be fired. Left with no income, many immigrants were arrested and interned.

"Once a German – Always a German!"

Propaganda poster
Around 1918

White folks, be they Scotch, Irish, English, American, or just plain Canadian, do not want to reside in the neighborhood of a colony which speaks the enemy language, adopts the costumes and customs of enemy countries.

Manitoba Free Press
October 5, 1918

The Suspension of Liberties

Between 1914 and 1920, the *War Measures Act* restricted civil liberties for hundreds of thousands of Canadians. It also imposed censorship, required registration for certain groups, and suspended freedom of expression and association, as well as legal protections.

The Act particularly affected Canadians from countries at war with the British Empire, who were labelled "enemy aliens." Around 8,500 of them were arrested and detained without cause or due process during this time.

❚❚ The man whose honour has been mistrusted, and who has been singled out for national humiliation, will remember it and sooner or later it will have to be atoned for. **❚❚**

Daily British Whig
September 8, 1917

Internees at the Castle Mountain camp, Alberta

1915

Registration Notices

These notices required "enemy aliens" to register with authorities, to help determine whether they posed a risk. More than 80,000 registered, and around 8,500 of these were interned. Two-thirds of the internees were of Ukrainian origin.

The reasons for internment were many and often arbitrary. They included being unemployed, breaking the law, or trying to leave the country.

DOMINION OF CANADA

GERMANS, AUSTRIANS, HUNGARIANS and TURKS
ATTENTION!

Every German, Austrian, Hungarian and Turk is hereby notified to report himself immediately at the Office of the Registrar for Alien Enemies, Toronto.

The Registration Office is at 34 Adelaide St. E., Toronto

The Registrar for Alien Enemies is E. COATSWORTH.

Telephone Main 7465.

DOMINION OF CANADA

DEUTSCHE, OESTREICHER, UNGARN und TÜRKEN
ACHTUNG!

Jeder Deutsche, Oestreicher, Ungar und Türke wird hierdurch aufgefordert sich sofort in dem Registrations Bureau dieses Bezirks zu melden.

Registrations Office ist 34 Adelaide St. E.

Registrator für Angehörige feindlicher Lauder E. Coatsworth
Telephone Main 7465.

Internment Camps and Receiving Stations in Canada, 1914–1920

Under the direction of the Office of Internment Operations, internees were delivered to more than 24 temporary detention centres and camps. This map indicates sites identified to date.

The last camps closed in February 1920, 15 months after the end of the war. Canada's first internment operations officially ceased in June 1920.

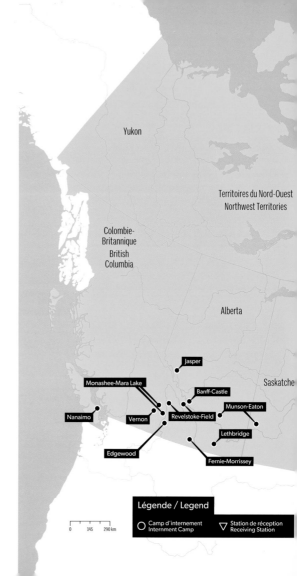

Yukon

Territoires du Nord-Ouest
Northwest Territories

Colombie-Britannique
British Columbia

Alberta

Saskatche

Jasper

Monashee-Mara Lake

Banff-Castle

Munson-Eaton

Nanaimo

Vernon

Revelstoke-Field

Lethbridge

Edgewood

Fernie-Morrissey

Légende / Legend

0   145   290 km

○ Camp d'internement
Internment Camp

▽ Station de réception
Receiving Station

Manitoba

Québec

Île-du-Prince-Édouard
Prince Edward Island

Winnipeg

Kapuskasing

Spirit Lake

Valcartier

Beauport

Amherst

Halifax

Ontario

Montréal

Sault Ste. Marie

Nouvelle-Écosse
Nova Scotia

Petawawa

Kingston

Nouveau-Brunswick
New Brunswick

Toronto

Niagara Falls

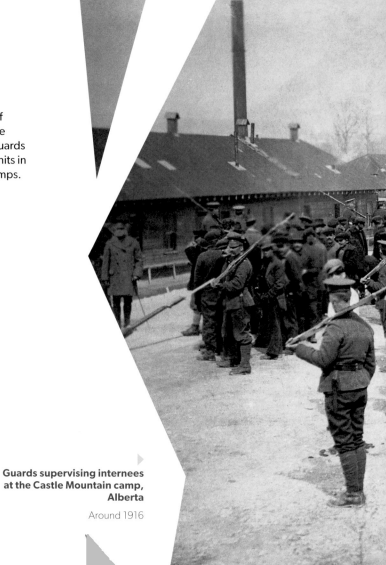

Guarding the Camps

The Department of Militia and Defence provided 2,000 guards to oversee work units in the internment camps.

Guards supervising internees at the Castle Mountain camp, Alberta

Around 1916

Categories of Internee

Reflecting international protocols and prejudices of the time, "first class" internees, largely German in origin, lived in better internment conditions than those considered "second class," who were primarily of Ukrainian origin. The government required the latter to undertake backbreaking labour, such as road construction and forestry.

Internees carrying out forestry work at the Kapuskasing camp, Ontario

1914–1920

Captive in Canada

Immigrant Oleksa Bilous was imprisoned in a Canadian internment camp when he made this diorama reflecting his Ukrainian origins.

In labour camps, Ukrainian internees rubbed shoulders with Serbs, Croats, Hungarians, Slovaks and Czechs, along with men from the Austro-Hungarian Empire, the Ottoman Empire and Bulgaria.

Worker Under Austrian Domination During the European War. In Canadian Captivity

Oleksa Bilous
Around 1917

Remnants of a Buried Past

These objects, discovered during recent archaeological digs at the Morrissey camp in British Columbia, are among the only remaining traces of the presence and daily lives of internees.

// This is giving a voice to individuals who have been essentially forgotten about." **//**

Sarah Beaulieu
Archaeologist
2015

▶

Tobacco Tin, Brick, Barbed Wire, Pipe and Buttons

Morrissey Camp, British Columbia
1915–1918

Captivity in Kapuskasing

This view of the Kapuskasing camp
in northern Ontario was painted by
an internee during captivity.

*Made During Wartime
at Internment Camp
Kapuskasing*

Unknown Artist
Kapuskasing, Ontario
1914–1920

George Forchuk:
Loss of Assets and Identity

George Forchuk left Ukraine and emigrated to Canada in 1913, at the age of 17. He was given 160 acres of land to clear in Alberta.

Arrested in 1915, he was one of a number of internees sent to the Jasper camp, in Alberta, to build the infrastructure for a future national park.

Forchuk successfully escaped from the camp and the backbreaking work, but had to change his identity in order to rebuild his life. The good farmland he had received was never returned.

> Even now, almost ninety years later, it still hurts me to talk about it. It affected him all his life. He lost his identity. He had to become someone else. I don't know to this day what Dad's original name was.
>
> **Marshall Forchuk**
> Son of George Forchuk
> 2006

George and Anna Forchuk on their wedding day

July 1920

Tunnelling to Freedom

An internee at the Morrissey camp, near Fernie, British Columbia, made this shovel to dig a tunnel with an eye to escape.

Escape attempts were dangerous. Of the 107 internees who died in captivity, six were killed while trying to escape.

**Shovel Made
by an Internee**

1915–1918

Mary Hancharuk Bayrak:
Born in an Internment Camp

Mary Hancharuk Bayrak was born on December 16, 1915 at the Spirit Lake camp, near Amos in Abitibi, Quebec. She spent the first eight months of her life there.

Given that her father Nikolaj was interned, lodgings were allocated to Mary, her mother Felicia, her grandmother Anna, and her brother Edward. Nikolaj was freed, with conditions, in August 1916.

❚❚ I thought it was a terrible thing to be in a camp. We thought it was for doing something wrong. We thought, we had come from someplace else and weren't liked and were put in a camp. I just never told anybody about it. **❚❚**

Mary Hancharuk Bayrak
2007

**Women and children
at Spirit Lake in Abitibi, Quebec**

1914–1918

The Families of Internees

At two camps — one in Vernon, British Columbia, and the other at Spirit Lake, Quebec — lodgings were built to house the 81 women and 156 children who had accompanied interned men.

Other families received a small amount of money to compensate for the loss of the main provider. It was often not enough — children were placed in orphanages, or had to go out to work.

Internees and their families at Spirit Lake in Abitibi, Quebec

1914–1918

Claudius Brown, Conscientious Objector

Originally from Grenada, in the West Indies, Claudius Brown was living in Winnipeg in 1918. When he was conscripted, he claimed the status of conscientious objector, without success. Although a small number of individuals belonging to specific religious group could claim this status, the courts did not recognize the Jehovah's Witnesses as a legitimate religious group.

Refusing to serve for religious reasons, Brown was sent to a military camp in Seaford, England, where he was tried and sentenced to a year in prison. Deemed "incorrigible," by his superior officers, Brown was freed on December 14, 1918.

I certify that this form has been read over to Pte. Brown C. and he refuses to sign it as a conscientious objector.

"Particulars of a Recruit"
Canadian Expeditionary Force
1918

**Claudius Brown
(bottom row, centre)**

Lands Expropriated for Greater Agricultural Production

The Kainai Nation, in Alberta, was one of many communities affected by a federal program aimed at increased agricultural production. Launched by the government in February 1918, the program involved the establishment of state-run farms on First Nations territory, along with the leasing of land to non-Indigenous farming families.

The program provided farmers of European descent with 90,000 acres of land that the Kainai Nation had refused to sell in 1916. Indigenous communities living on the territory were dispossessed.

Farmers of the Kainai Nation, in Fort MacLeod, Alberta

1915

02

The Second World War: Liberty Controlled

A Commitment to Total War

On September 10, 1939, Canada entered the war of its own volition, having gained its independence from Great Britain in foreign affairs.

This time, the government was better prepared than it had been in 1914. Under Prime Minister Mackenzie King, preventative measures were rapidly put in place. A week before Canada entered the war, the *War Measures Act* was invoked once again, and the *Defence of Canada Regulations* were adopted to meet any threat.

"CAR TON BRAS ...SAIT PORTER L'ÉPÉE"

> I appeal to my fellow Canadians to unite in a national effort to save from destruction all that makes life itself worth living, and to preserve for future generations those liberties and institutions which others have bequeathed to us.
>
> **William Lyon Mackenzie King**
> Prime Minister of Canada
> September 3, 1939

Recruitment Poster

1940

Controlling the Media

The government used the media to spread its messages. The *Defence of Canada Regulations* gave the government the power to censor the press and to ban, under threat of fines and imprisonment, anything that might imperil national security or the war effort.

// In times of peace, people will not stand for the strict police surveillance and curtailment of civil liberty that become necessary in crises such as the present. **//**

The Hamilton Spectator
June 11, 1940

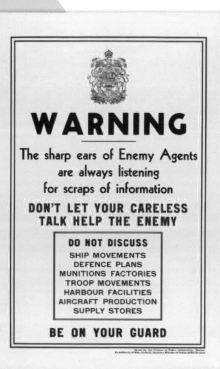

WARNING

The sharp ears of Enemy Agents are always listening for scraps of information

DON'T LET YOUR CARELESS TALK HELP THE ENEMY

DO NOT DISCUSS

SHIP MOVEMENTS
DEFENCE PLANS
MUNITIONS FACTORIES
TROOP MOVEMENTS
HARBOUR FACILITIES
AIRCRAFT PRODUCTION
SUPPLY STORES

BE ON YOUR GUARD

Wartime National Security Poster

1939–1941

Intensifying Prejudice

Following the entry of Italy (1940) and Japan (1941) into the war on the side of Germany, newspapers enhanced fear, prejudice, and discrimination toward Canadians of Italian and Japanese origin.

Ad for a Victory Bonds Campaign

1942

A Well-Oiled Machine

The *War Measures Act* allowed the Royal Canadian Mounted Police (RCMP) to carry out its work with few restrictions. The police drew up lists of suspects and made arrests, following approval by a federal advisory board. The legal system largely supported the emergency measures now in place.

▶
"To Male Enemy Aliens, Notice"

1942

Citizen Rallies

A number of associations defending civil liberties were active during the war. The Civil Liberties Association of Toronto even organized rallies that attracted thousands of people.

The Association closely observed the application of the *Defence of Canada Regulations* and agitated for the restoration of banned organizations.

Notice for Citizens' Rally at Maple Leaf Gardens in Toronto

July 17, 1942

Another War,
Other Target Groups

Invocation of the *War Measures Act* in 1939 affected tens of thousands of Canadians. Once again, residents from countries at war with Canada were particularly affected.

In the accounts that follow, we explore the troubling consequences of these measures on people of German, Italian and Japanese origin, displaced Chippewa families, and a political prisoner.

**Raymond Moriyama
and his mother Elsie Nobuko,
at the Slocan camp
in British Columbia**

Spring 1943

Adventures Behind Barbed Wire

In 1939, Otto Ellmaurer, who had lived in Canada for 10 years, was arrested and accused by the RCMP of belonging to a pro-Nazi group. He produced humorous scenes of his internment at the Kananaskis camp in Alberta.

Out of 600,000 Canadians of German origin, around 850 were interned during the Second World War. By 1942, most of them had been freed, due to a lack of incriminating evidence.

Humoristishche Erlebnisse Hinterm Drahtverhau Konzentration (Comical Adventures Behind Barbed Wire)

Otto Ellmaurer
Kananaskis, Alberta
Around 1939

Leo und seine Künstler! (Leo and His Artists!)

Otto Ellmaurer
Kananaskis, Alberta
Around 1939

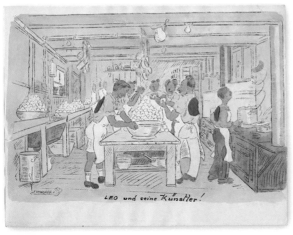

Veterans Guard of Canada

Guard duties in the internment camps
were undertaken primarily by veterans
of the First World War, who were
considered too old to serve overseas.

**Inspection parade at
Kananaskis camp,
Alberta**

February 24, 1940

Vincenzo Poggi:
A Captive Artist

Painter Vincenzo Poggi, who had been in Canada since 1929, was one of the 500 people from the Italian-Canadian community interned during the Second World War. His arrest in 1940 may have been tied to his role at a press service that acted as a propaganda agency for Fascist Italy.

Interned in the camps at Petawawa, Ontario, and Fredericton, New Brunswick, Poggi was given a conditional release in 1943. He was required to report to the RCMP each month, and to avoid any Fascist activity.

> I was interned at Petawawa on the 6th January 1942. Fascist leaders within the camp refused to allow me living quarters in hut 11 (because) I was not a good fascist and only good fascists were desired in that particular hut.
>
> **Vincenzo Poggi**
> Around 1943

Vincenzo Poggi's bag lists the places and years of his detention, and features the red circle traditionally associated with the uniform for prisoners of war.

Vincenzo Poggi's Bag

Around 1943

Communist Internee

S. G. Neil, a Finnish Canadian from Sudbury, Ontario, was one of a hundred individuals interned following the outlawing of the Communist Party of Canada in 1940.

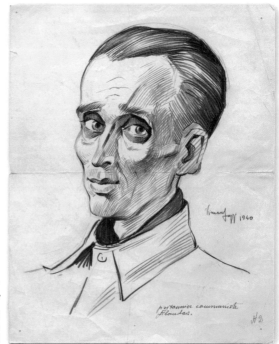

Communist Prisoner

By Vincenzo Poggi
Petawawa, Ontario
1940

Sandra Corbo:
A Stolen Childhood

Following the internment of her grandfather and her uncle Nicola, two-year-old Sandra Corbo and her parents moved from Toronto to Montréal to help support the extended family. Because both her father and mother had to work, Sandra was placed in an orphanage for two years.

Seventy years later, she noted that this traumatic experience had marked her for life.

> **II** I'm 73 and it still hurts like hell. It was a shame brought on the family. The feeling of not being worthy. Of being considered a traitor. It's the public perception reflected back on you. **II**
>
> **Sandra Corbo**
> 2011

Sandra Corbo (left)

Mary Murakami Kitagawa's "Journey Through Hell"

Japan's attack on Pearl Harbor, in December 1941, transformed the lives of tens of thousands of Canadians of Japanese origin.

In 1942, the *War Measures Act* was invoked to force more than 21,000 Canadians of Japanese origin — 75% of whom were Canadian nationals — to move a minimum of 160 kilometres from the West Coast.

The farm and dwelling of the father of seven-year-old Mary Murakami Kitagawa were seized and sold. Forced to move ten times between 1942 and 1946, the family was subjected to difficult conditions in the camps of British Columbia, and hard labour on the beet farms of Alberta.

The farm belonging to Mary Murakami Kitagawa's parents was never returned. In 1946, the family settled in Magrath, Alberta.

> My family was swept away from our home in this storm of hatred. Our journey through incarceration was brutal and dehumanizing.
>
> **Mary Murakami Kitagawa**
> 2019

Mary Murakami Kitagawa (second from left)

Ganges, British Columbia
1940

Stripped of Their Assets

Stripped of his assets, Mary Murakami Kitagawa's father made *getas* in the camp. His children wore them throughout the summer, in order to save their shoes for the rest of the year.

Getas

Made by Katsuyori Murakami
1942–1945

Dispersal or Deportation

Toward the end of the war, the government required Canadians of Japanese origin to either settle east of the Rockies, or sign documents confirming their deportation to Japan after the conflict ended. Around 4,000 people — half of whom had been born in Canada — left for Japan in 1946.

Canadians of Japanese origin who were interned during the Second World War, then deported to Japan

Slocan, British Columbia
1946

Norman Takeuchi:
A Difficult Past

The work *A Measured Act* by artist Norman Takeuchi, born in Vancouver in 1937, reflects the experiences of the 21,000 Canadians of Japanese origin — including the artist and his family — who were forcibly displaced into isolated communities and internment camps.

Composed of five life-sized paper kimonos and drawings with Conté crayon, the work also reflects the artist's own lengthy reconciliation with his Japanese heritage.

❚❚ As a member of a community that experienced the upheaval of the internment years, my artwork embraces conflicting views: the earlier difficulties of acknowledging my Japanese heritage, and the later acceptance of it. **❚❚**

Norman Takeuchi
2019

**Ken Takeuchi (left),
Bob Takeuchi (centre)
and Norman Takeuchi (right)**

1947

Shirt of the
rising sun
So red and full
on my back
A moving target.

A Measured Act – Angler

By Norman Takeuchi
Acrylic, Conté crayon and oil pastel
2006

Stony Point and the Displacement of Chippewa Families

In 1942, the Department of National Defence used the *War Measures Act* to expropriate the Stony Point reserve — 35 kilometres north of Sarnia, in southern Ontario — to build the Ipperwash military base. Some 20 Chippewa families were forcibly relocated to the Kettle Point reserve. Decades of protest followed in an effort to recover their lost territory.

> We don't side [with] Hitler and his heartless aid [e]s. [All] we [want is] to keep Stony Point for our descendant [s]. I am the oldest, and have [the right] to say something about our poor children's inheritance.

Mrs Beattie Greenbird
Band Elder
and Kettle Point resident
April 24, 1942

A house being moved from Stony Point to Kettle Point, Ontario

1942

Camillien Houde, Political Prisoner

In August 1940, Camillien Houde, Mayor of Montréal, publicly opposed the new *National Resources Mobilization Act*. Under the Act, everyone 16 or older was required to be listed on a national registry, with the aim of fully mobilizing the workforce.

Arrested by the RCMP, Houde spent four years in internment camps at Petawawa, Ontario, and Fredericton, New Brunswick. Freed on August 16, 1944, he returned to Montréal a hero.

> The difference between internment and jail is that one can be interned for the duration of the war, while prison has a fixed sentence. Not knowing the length of one's captivity is torture.
>
> **Camillien Houde**
> Letter to his wife
> August 7, 1940

Camillien Houde

1930s

Prisoner of War No. 694

As this badge indicates, Camillien Houde was identified as prisoner of war no. 694 at the camp in Petawawa, Ontario, where he was detained from 1940 to 1942.

**Camillien Houde's
Camp Badge**

Around 1942

The October Crisis
and the Dawn of a New Era

At the end of the 1960s, both Quebec and the
wider world were undergoing massive upheaval,
both peaceful and violent, reflecting a keen
desire for change.

Jouez Québec
(***Let's Play, Quebec***)

Vinyl record by Robert Charlebois
1969

BEFORE . . .

Workmen are shown putting protective boarding over the Seven-Up plant windows on Graham blvd. (on the advice of the Town Police) prior to Tuesday evening's riots.

RIGHT: Asst. Chief Georges Pigeon and Police Chief Walter Boyle keep close to demonstrators.

ABOVE left, broken window in the Post Office on Graham blvd. and, at right, mailbox pushed through Laniel Amusement window at Rockland and Beaumont.

BELOW, the battered relic of a radio car after the mobsters had wreaked havoc on it. The rioters battered the occupant, tried to set fire to the car and then rocked it furiously, trying vainly to overturn it. This was directly opposite The Weekly Post office on Dunbar ave.

DURING . . .

Demonstrators marching away from Seven-Up plant after throwing Molotov cocktails at the building.

Burning picket signs are shown above as demonstration comes to an end.

"Mainly because"
. . . it was there!

Dollar signs in smashed Dominion Store window do NOT indicate savings - for Dominion.

A violent strike at the 7UP factory in Town of Mount Royal

February 29, 1968

03

Firestorm in October 1970

The 1970 October Crisis marked the third invocation of the *War Measures Act*, and the first in peacetime. The Front de libération du Québec (FLQ), a revolutionary movement seeking Quebec independence, carried out two political kidnappings — something never before seen in North America. Governments and majority public opinion demanded a decisive response, although protesters were alarmed by the suspension of civil liberties.

Small boy walking alongside military vehicles

November 1970

Front de libération du Québec: Independence, Socialism, Revolution

Formed in 1963, the FLQ sought Quebec independence and a socialist state.

By 1970, it had carried out more than 200 bombings, in addition to thefts of weapons, explosives and money. In addition to causing the deaths of nine people, the FLQ put the country on high alert with the kidnapping of British diplomat James Cross on October 5, and the kidnapping of Quebec Minister Pierre Laporte on October 10. The discovery of Laporte's body on October 17 shocked Canadians everywhere.

> // The Front de libération du Québec wants the total independence of all Québécois, united in a free society, purged forever of the clique of voracious sharks, the patronizing `big bosses' and their henchmen who have made Quebec their hunting preserve for `cheap labour' and unscrupulous exploitation. //
>
> **FLQ Manifesto**
> October 1970

▶

First Page of the FLQ Manifesto

October 1970

front de libération du québec

MANIFESTE

Le Front de Libération du Québec n'est pas le messie, ni un Robin des bois des temps modernes. C'est un regroupement de travailleurs québécois qui sont décidés à tout mettre en oeuvre pour que le peuple du Québec prenne définitivement en mains son destin.

Le Front de Libération du Québec veut l'indépendance totale des Québécois, réunis dans une société libre et purgée à jamais de sa clique de requins voraces, les "big-boss" patronneux et leurs valets qui ont fait du Québec leur chasse-gardée du cheap labor et de l'exploitation sans scrupules.

Le Front de Libération du Québec n'est pas un mouvement d'agression, mais la réponse à une agression, celle organisée par la haute finance par l'entremise des marionnettes des gouvernements fédéral et provincial (le show de la Brinks, le bill 63, la carte électorale, la taxe dite de " progrès social" (sic), power corporation, l'assurance-médecins, les gars de Lapalme ...).

Le Front de Libération du Québec s'auto-finance d'impôts volontaires (sic) pré-levés à même les entreprises d'exploitation des ouvriers (banques, compagnies de finance, etc ...)

Government of Quebec: Negotiation and Heartbreak

Quebec's government, led by Robert Bourassa, was shaken by the kidnapping of James Cross on October 5, and traumatized by that of Labour Minister Pierre Laporte five days later. How could the two lives be saved? Negotiate with the kidnappers? Fight them, no matter the cost?

> **//** They start with meetings. After that they have recourse to bombs, and now the kidnappings. So we have to stop that, because where will it finish? It is not a question of limiting the civil liberties of the people. It is a question of saving democracy. **//**
>
> **Robert Bourassa**
> Quebec Premier
> Interview on CBC Radio
> October 16, 1970

Autumn Hostage

Sculpture in homage to Pierre Laporte
By William Hodd McElcheran
After 1970

The City of Montréal:
"For the Protection of Society"

Montréal was in turmoil by the late 1960s. Strikes and demonstrations intensified, and often turned violent. Capitalism was denounced, as were Anglo-American domination, the Vietnam War, and a host of other causes. Mayor Drapeau's own home was bombed.

The epicentre of the October Crisis was Montréal. Police were exhausted and overwhelmed. But the silent majority supported Jean Drapeau. In the municipal elections of October 25, 1970, he won 92% of the votes and every last seat.

> The assistance of higher levels of government has become essential for the protection of society against the seditious plot and the apprehended insurrection.
>
> **Jean Drapeau**
> Mayor of Montréal
> Letter to Prime Minister
> Pierre Elliott Trudeau
> October 15, 1970

Soldiers patrolling in front of Montréal's city hall

October 16, 1970

The Canadian Government: A Forceful Response

The *War Measures Act* took effect at dawn on October 16, 1970. The House of Commons ratified it by an overwhelming majority of 190 to 16.

The Act was invoked in response to written requests from Quebec and the City of Montréal, which feared a state of insurrection.

> The *War Measures Act* gives sweeping powers to the Government. [...] They are necessary, however, to permit the police to deal with persons who advocate or promote the violent overthrow of our democratic system.
>
> **Pierre Elliott Trudeau**
> Prime Minister of Canada
> October 16, 1970

▶

Pierre Elliott Trudeau
Prime Minister of Canada
October 18, 1970

Mobilizing the Forces of Law and Order

On October 15, the day before the *War Measures Act* was invoked, the Quebec government asked the army to intervene under the *National Defence Act*. About 12,000 troops were deployed in Quebec and Ottawa. They remained there until January 4, 1971.

Their missions: to protect VIPs, guard strategic installations and reassure the population.

In addition, an unprecedented decree by the Bourassa government designated the Sûreté du Québec in charge of all the province's police forces, some 13,000 men.

// In the short term and until the immediate threat is contained, there is no doubt that extraordinary physical security measures are necessary and effective. **//**

John Starnes
Director General of the Royal Canadian
Mounted Police Security Service
October 22, 1970

Canadian Army Ballistic Helmet
1960s

Public Opinion:
Trust in the Authorities

A significant majority, both in Quebec and in Canada as a whole, supported the implementation of war measures. A public opinion poll in mid-December 1970 revealed overwhelming 87% support — the highest ever recorded for a government decision. Equally revealing was that, by December 18, 1970, the office of Prime Minister Trudeau had received 12,000 letters and telegrams. Fewer than 2% criticized the federal government's actions.

> **//** Quebec is sitting on a volcano. This is no longer the time to wrap oneself in the great and the good principles of democracy. We must have confidence in those elected by the people. [...] There will always be a time to point out errors, if errors there be. [...] It is our freedom that is at stake. **//**
>
> **Sylvio Saint-Amant**
> *Le Nouvelliste*
> October 17, 1970

Newsstand in Montréal

October 1970

Protest:
The End Does Not Justify the Means

Although a minority position in both Quebec and Canada, criticism of the use of war measures was forcefully expressed by members of Quebec's young intellectual left, who were largely separatist.

There were dissenting voices in anglophone Canada as well. Supporting neither the FLQ nor Quebec separatism, they nonetheless demanded that fundamental freedoms be upheld.

> We are not prepared to use the preservation of law and order as a smokescreen to destroy the liberties and the freedom of the people of Canada. [...] The government, I submit, is using a sledgehammer to crack a peanut.
>
> **Tommy Douglas**
> Leader of the New Democratic Party of Canada
> October 16, 1970

Le Quartier latin

Université de Montréal student newspaper
November 7, 1970

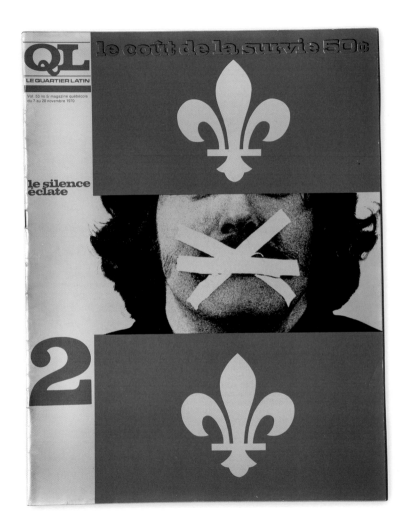

Arrests and Police Raids

Beginning on Friday, October 16, 1970, following the imposition of the *War Measures Act*, police launched a series of arrests. More than 500 people were imprisoned — some for a few hours; others for several months. Very few were tried, and only a handful were found guilty.

The police also carried out more than 30,000 raids. Everyone lived through the same political crisis, but each experience was deeply personal.

❚❚ My son is in prison
And I feel within myself
In my very depths
For the first time
In spite of myself, in spite of myself
Between flesh and bone
Rage setting in **❚❚**

Félix Leclerc
"L'alouette en colère"
("The Angry Skylark")
1970

▶

**Corridor of stacked cells
at Parthenais Prison**

The Singer and the Poet

Pauline Julien (1928–1998) was a singer known for her passion, her feminism, and her support for Quebec independence. Her partner, poet and future politician Gérald Godin (1938–1994), was also director of the publishing company Parti pris, as well as a contributor to the popular weekly *Québec-Presse*.

The couple was imprisoned for eight days, then released without charge. After she was freed, Pauline Julien was astonished to return to an empty home. Her children (ages 15 and 18), three of their friends, and Julien's sister had also been picked up by the police.

> **❚❚** hey, pacifists
> hey, those who remain silent
> hey, where are most of you
> from the depths of prisons
> from the depths of injustice
> they cry out to you **❚❚**
>
> **Pauline Julien**
> "Eille" ("Hey")
> 1971

Gérald Godin and Pauline Julien
1969

In Every Struggle

Michel Chartrand (1916–2010) was a key figure within the Confédération des syndicats nationaux, a large and powerful trade union. He was involved in every labour, social and political struggle.

Known for his socialist stance and colourful language, he was arrested on October 16, 1970 and spent four months in prison.

Simonne Monet-Chartrand, a feminist activist and pacificist, ran herself ragged during her husband's incarceration. She gave several talks and interviews, and made numerous public appeals, in addition to managing the family home.

> There is certainly bad faith, ill will, negligence, incompetence, and poor administration. I know of nothing more badly managed than justice in Quebec.
>
> **Michel Chartrand**
> Statement at his trial
> February 1, 1971

Simonne Monet-Chartrand with Michel Chartrand upon his release from prison

February 16, 1971

Doctor and Activist

Serge Mongeau (1937–) is a public health physician known for his books and popular broadcasts. He was also an activist within the Mouvement pour la défense des prisonniers politiques québécois ("Movement for the Defence of Quebec Political Prisoners"), which ensured that former members of the FLQ received justice. Arrested while driving, he was detained for a week.

I am a 'prisoner of war', in a war that was never technically declared, but whose proclamation allows authorities to worsen the existing long-term repression. I am behind bars without knowing why.

Serge Mongeau
Open letter to Robert Bourassa,
Premier of Quebec
October 30, 1970

**Serge Mongeau (right)
and Pauline Julien (left)**

December 12, 1970

A Man for All Seasons

Nick Auf der Maur (1942–1998) was a multifaceted anglophone Montréaler. At the *Montreal Star*, the CBC, and the alternative magazine *The Last Post*, he had cultivated numerous contacts.

He also knew members of the FLQ, and was imprisoned for four days, based on friendships authorities viewed as questionable. Like many anglophones, he protested the implementation of war measures.

> **❚❚** Up until that point […]
> I always had a vague assumption that
> the police, if not the authorities, acted on good
> faith, that they were really only after people they
> thought guilty. Now I had a very different
> feeling. They're out to get everybody. **❚❚**
>
> **Nick Auf der Maur**
> "Memoirs of a Prisoner of War"
> *The Last Post*
> November 1970

Nick Auf der Maur
February 11, 1972

Disruptive Ideas

Producer Jacques Larue-Langlois (1934– 2001) held radical convictions, although he was personally non-violent. Radio-Canada fired him for his ideas in 1968.

He went on to establish the Agence de presse libre du Québec ("Quebec Free Press Agency"), as a voice for protest groups. Arrested on October 16, 1970, he was not released until June 16, 1971.

> against the unbelievable
> folly of war measures
> against the eloquent pigheadedness
> of the wealthy
> against the ignorance that held back our forebears
> against the ludicrous concrete of my prison walls
> against the burning hunger in my belly
> against privations that have not yet ended
> against the endless desert to which
> they've brought me

Jacques Larue-Langlois
"Soixante-treizième jour"
("Seventy-Third Day")
1971

Jacques Larue-Langlois with raised fist, celebrating his acquittal. To his right: Robert Lemieux and Charles Gagnon, two of his co-accused in the Trial of the Montréal Five. To his left is his son Renaud.

June 16, 1971

Epilogue: A Long Road

The state of civil liberties in Canada has continued to evolve since 1970. Communities and individuals affected by the *War Measures Act* have helped effect change. These freedoms remain fragile, however, despite solemn pronouncements and new laws that reflect tangible progress.

Canadian Charter of Rights and Freedoms

April 17, 1982

CANADIAN CHARTER OF RIGHTS AND FREEDOMS

Whereas Canada is founded upon principles that recognize the supremacy of God and the rule of law:

Guarantee of Rights and Freedoms

1. The *Canadian Charter of Rights and Freedoms* guarantees the rights and freedoms set out in it subject only to such reasonable limits prescribed by law as can be demonstrably justified in a free and democratic society.

Fundamental Freedoms

2. Everyone has the following fundamental freedoms: *(a)* freedom of conscience and religion; *(b)* freedom of thought, belief, opinion and expression, including freedom of the press and other media of communication; *(c)* freedom of peaceful assembly; and *(d)* freedom of association.

Democratic Rights

3. Every citizen of Canada has the right to vote in an election of members of the House of Commons or of a legislative assembly and to be qualified for membership therein. 4.(1) No House of Commons and no legislative assembly shall continue for longer than five years from the date fixed for the return of the writs at a general election of its members. (2) In time of real or apprehended war, invasion or insurrection, a House of Commons may be continued by Parliament and a legislative assembly may be continued by the legislature beyond five years if such continuation is not opposed by the votes of more than one-third of the members of the House of Commons or the legislative assembly, as the case may be. 5. There shall be a sitting of Parliament and of each legislature at least once every twelve months.

Mobility Rights

6.(1) Every citizen of Canada has the right to enter, remain in and leave Canada. (2) Every citizen of Canada and every person who has the status of a permanent resident of Canada has the right *(a)* to move to and take up residence in any province; and *(b)* to pursue the gaining of a livelihood in any province. (3) The rights specified in subsection (2) are subject to *(a)* any laws or practices of general application in force in a province other than those that discriminate among persons primarily on the basis of province of present or previous residence; and *(b)* any laws providing for reasonable residency requirements as a qualification for the receipt of publicly provided social services. (4) Subsections (2) and (3) do not preclude any law, program or activity that has as its object the amelioration in a province of conditions of ndividuals in that province who are socially or economically disadvantaged f the rate of employment in that province is below the rate of employment in Canada.

Legal Rights

7. Everyone has the right to life, liberty and security of the person and he right not to be deprived thereof except in accordance with the principles of fundamental justice. 8. Everyone has the right to be secure against nreasonable search or seizure. 9. Everyone has the right not to be arbitrarily letained or imprisoned. 10. Everyone has the right on arrest or detention *(a)* o be informed promptly of the reasons therefor; *(b)* to retain and instruct ounsel without delay and to be informed of that right; and *(c)* to have he validity of the detention determined by way of *habeas corpus* and to be eleased if the detention is not lawful. 11. Any person charged with an offence as the right *(a)* to be informed without unreasonable delay of the specific ffence; *(b)* to be tried within a reasonable time; *(c)* not to be compelled to e a witness in proceedings against that person in respect of the offence; *(d)* o be presumed innocent until proven guilty according to law in a fair and ublic hearing by an independent and impartial tribunal; *(e)* not to be denied easonable bail without just cause; *(f)* except in the case of an offence under nilitary law tried before a military tribunal, to the benefit of trial by jury here the maximum punishment for the offence is imprisonment for five ears or a more severe punishment; *(g)* not to be found guilty on account of ny act or omission unless, at the time of the act or omission, it constituted n offence under Canadian or international law or was criminal according to e general principles of law recognized by the community of nations; *(h)* if nally acquitted of the offence, not to be tried for it again and, if finally found uilty and punished for the offence, not to be tried or punished for it again; and *(i)* if found guilty of the offence and if the punishment for the offence has been varied between the time of commission and the time of sentencing, to the benefit of the lesser punishment. 12. Everyone has the right not to be subjected to any cruel and unusual treatment or punishment. 13. A witness who testifies in any proceedings has the right not to have any incriminating evidence so given used to incriminate that witness in any other proceedings, except in a prosecution for perjury or for the giving of contradictory evidence. 14. A party or witness in any proceedings who does not understand or speak the language in which the proceedings are conducted or who is deaf has the right to the assistance of an interpreter.

Equality Rights

15.(1) Every individual is equal before and under the law and has the right to the equal protection and equal benefit of the law without discrimination and, in particular, without discrimination based on race, national or ethnic origin, colour, religion, sex, age or mental or physical disability. (2) Subsection (1) does not preclude any law, program or activity that has as its object the amelioration of conditions of disadvantaged individuals or groups including those that are disadvantaged because of race, national or ethnic origin, colour, religion, sex, age or mental or physical disability.

Official Languages of Canada

16.(1) English and French are the official languages of Canada and have equality of status and equal rights and privileges as to their use in all institutions of the Parliament and government of Canada. (2) English and French are the official languages of New Brunswick and have equality of status and equal rights and privileges as to their use in all institutions of the legislature and government of New Brunswick. (3) Nothing in this Charter limits the authority of Parliament or a legislature to advance the equality of status or use of English and French. 16.1(1) The English linguistic community and the French linguistic community in New Brunswick have equality of status and equal rights and privileges, including the right to distinct educational institutions and such distinct cultural institutions as are necessary for the preservation and promotion of those communities. (2) The role of the legislature and government of New Brunswick to preserve and promote the status, rights and privileges referred to in subsection (1) is affirmed. 17.(1) Everyone has the right to use English or French in any debates and other proceedings of Parliament. (2) Everyone has the right to use English or French in any debates and other proceedings of the legislature of New Brunswick.18. (1) The statutes, records and journals of Parliament shall be printed and published in English and French and both language versions are equally authoritative. (2) The statutes, records and journals of the legislature of New Brunswick shall be printed and published in English and French and both language versions are equally authoritative.19.(1) Either English or French may be used by any person in, or in any pleading in or process issuing from, any court established by Parliament. (2) Either English or French may be used by any person in, or in any pleading in or process issuing from, any court of New Brunswick. 20.(1) Any member of the public in Canada has the right to communicate with, and to receive available services from, any head or central office of an institution of the Parliament or government of Canada in English or French, and has the same right with respect to any other office of any such institution where *(a)* there is a significant demand for communications with and services from that office in such language; or *(b)* due to the nature of the office, it is reasonable that communications with and services from that office be available in both English and French. (2) Any member of the public in New Brunswick has the right to communicate with, and to receive available services from, any office of an institution of the legislature or government of New Brunswick in English or French. 21. Nothing in sections 16 to 20 abrogates or derogates from any right, privilege or obligation with respect to the English and French languages, or either of them, that exists or is continued by virtue of any other provision of the Constitution of Canada.22. Nothing in sections 16 to 20 abrogates or derogates from any legal or customary right or privilege acquired or enjoyed either before or after the coming into force of this Charter with respect to any language that is not English or French.

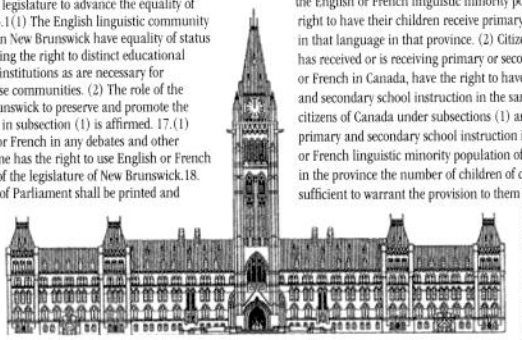

Minority Language Educational Rights

23.(1) Citizens of Canada *(a)* whose first language learned and still understood is that of the English or French linguistic minority population of the province in which they reside, or *(b)* who have received their primary school instruction in Canada in English or French and reside in a province where the language in which they received that instruction is the language of the English or French linguistic minority population of the province, have the right to have their children receive primary and secondary school instruction in that language in that province. (2) Citizens of Canada of whom any child has received or is receiving primary or secondary school instruction in English or French in Canada, have the right to have all their children receive primary and secondary school instruction in the same language. (3) The right of citizens of Canada under subsections (1) and (2) to have their children receive primary and secondary school instruction in the language of the English or French linguistic minority population of a province *(a)* applies wherever in the province the number of children of citizens who have such a right is sufficient to warrant the provision to them out of public funds of minority language instruction; and *(b)* includes, where the number of those children so warrants, the right to have them receive that instruction in minority language educational facilities provided out of public funds.

Enforcement

24.(1) Anyone whose rights or freedoms, as guaranteed by this Charter, have been infringed or denied may apply to a court of competent jurisdiction to obtain such remedy as the court considers appropriate and just in the circumstances. (2) Where, in proceedings under subsection (1),a court concludes that evidence was obtained in a manner that infringed or denied any rights or freedoms guaranteed by this Charter, the evidence shall be excluded if it is established that, having regard to all the circumstances, the admission of it in the proceedings would bring the administration of justice into disrepute.

General

25. The guarantee in this Charter of certain rights and freedoms shall not be construed so as to abrogate or derogate from any aboriginal, treaty or other rights or freedoms that pertain to the aboriginal peoples of Canada including *(a)* any rights or freedoms that have been recognized by the Royal Proclamation of October 7, 1763; and *(b)* any rights or freedoms that now exist by way of land claims agreements or may be so acquired. 26. The guarantee in this Charter of certain rights and freedoms shall not be construed as denying the existence of any other rights or freedoms that exist in Canada. 27. This Charter shall be interpreted in a manner consistent with the preservation and enhancement of the multicultural heritage of Canadians. 28. Notwithstanding anything in this Charter, the rights and freedoms referred to in it are guaranteed equally to male and female persons. 29. Nothing in this Charter abrogates or derogates from any rights or privileges guaranteed by or under the Constitution of Canada in respect of denominational, separate or dissentient schools. 30. A reference in this Charter to a province or to the legislative assembly or legislature of a province shall be deemed to include a reference to the Yukon Territory and the Northwest Territories, or to the appropriate legislative authority thereof, as the case may be. 31. Nothing in this Charter extends the legislative powers of any body or authority.

Application of Charter

32.(1) This Charter applies (a) to the Parliament and government of Canada in respect of all matters within the authority of Parliament including all matters relating to the Yukon Territory and Northwest Territories; and (b) to the legislature and government of each province in respect of all matters within the authority of the legislature of each province. (2) Notwithstanding subsection (1), section 15 shall not have effect until three years after this section comes into force. 33.(1) Parliament or the legislature of a province may expressly declare in an Act of Parliament or of the legislature, as the case may be, that the Act or a provision thereof shall operate notwithstanding a provision included in section 2 or sections 7 to 15 of this Charter. (2) An Act or a provision of an Act in respect of which a declaration made under this section is in effect shall have such operation as it would have but for the provision of this Charter referred to in the declaration. (3) A declaration made under subsection (1) shall cease to have effect five years after it comes into force or on such earlier date as may be specified in the declaration.(4) Parliament or the legislature of a province may re-enact a declaration made under subsection (1).(5) Subsection (3) applies in respect of a re-enactment made under subsection (4).

Citation

34. This Part may be cited as the *Canadian Charter of Rights and Freedoms*.

" We must now establish the basic principles, the basic values and beliefs which hold us together as Canadians so that beyond our regional loyalties there is a way of life and a system of values which make us proud of the country that has given us such freedom and such immeasurable joy."

P.E. Trudeau 1981

1988

Replacement of the *War Measures Act* with the *Emergency Measures Act*

> **❚❚** Never again will there be the ability to use the *War Measures Act* to knock on the door in the dark of night, to sweep up our citizens, to hold them without charge and without the right to *habeas corpus.* **❚❚**
>
> **Perrin Beatty**
> Canadian Minister of National Defence
> July 11, 1988

▶

First page of the *Emergency Measures Act*

1988

ch. 29

C-77

Second Session, Thirty-third Parliament,
35-36-37 Elizabeth II, 1986-87-88

THE HOUSE OF COMMONS OF CANADA

BILL C-77

An Act to authorize the taking of special temporary measures to ensure safety and security during national emergencies and to amend other Acts in consequence thereof

---

AS PASSED BY THE HOUSE OF COMMONS APRIL 27, 1988

C-77

Deuxième session, trente-troisième législature,
35-36-37 Elizabeth II, 1986-87-88

CHAMBRE DES COMMUNES DU CANADA

PROJET DE LOI C-77

Loi visant à autoriser à titre temporaire des mesures extraordinaires de sécurité en situation de crise nationale et à modifier d'autres lois en conséquence

---

ADOPTÉ PAR LA CHAMBRE DES COMMUNES LE 27 AVRIL 1988

1988

Signature of the Japanese Canadian Redress Agreement

> The redress agreement will remain a significant moment [...], an unusual achievement by a small group of citizens who, because of a nation's violation of their citizenship rights, launched a movement to negotiate a settlement with the federal government.

Roy Miki
Literature professor, relocated in childhood, and one of the negotiators of the Agreement
2004

Signature of the Japanese Canadian Redress Agreement, by the president of the National Association of Japanese Canadians, Art Miki, and Prime Minister Brian Mulroney

September 22, 1988

2005

Passing of the *Internment of Persons of Ukrainian Origin Recognition Act*

> **❝** This is a historic day not only for the over one million Ukrainian Canadians, but also for Canada as a society. **❞**
>
> **Inky Mark**
> Member of Parliament and author of the Act

▶

Interned Madonna

By John Boxtel
Spirit Lake Camp, Quebec
2011

2016

Stony Point :
Ceding of Ipperwash lands by
the Department of National Defence

❚❚ Today, WWII is finally over for the Chippewas of Kettle and Stony Point with the closure of the taking of our lands in 1942. We look forward to a better relationship with Canada going forward, and today marks a new beginning. **❚❚**

Thomas Bressette
Chief of the Chippewas of Kettle and Stony Point First Nation
April 14, 2016

▶

Minister of National Defence Harjit Sajjan, Minister of Indigenous and Northern Affairs Carolyn Bennett, and Chief Thomas Bressette, at the signature of the agreement with the Kettle and Stony Point First Nation

April 14, 2016

2018

Expression of Regret
by the Royal Canadian Mounted Police
to the Italian-Canadian community

> **"** It began to heal the shame and affirmed that we are not forgotten. Someone is listening. **"**
>
> **Joyce Pillarella**
> Historian and granddaughter
> of internee Nicola Germano
> 2018

**Ceremonial expression of regret
by the RCMP to the Italian-Canadian
community**

Ottawa
September 18, 2018

2020

Refusal of the House of Commons to offer an apology for invocation of the *War Measures Act* and Army intervention in 1970

// The federal government [...] must show compassion to the 497 Quebec citizens and their families who were terrorized, and who have had to live with the legacy of these acts of aggression. It was unforgivable 50 years ago, and remains so today. **//**

Yves-François Blanchet
Leader of the Bloc québécois
October 29, 2020

▶

Liberté (Freedom)

By Marcel Barbeau
Maison Ludger-Duvernay
Montréal, Quebec
2010

CONTRIBUTIONS

We would like to thank the members of the core exhibition team for **Lost Liberties – The *War Measures Act*:** Chantal Baril, Julie Guinard, Jean-François Léger and Cathy Mitchell.

We would also like to express our appreciation for the members of communities affected by the *War Measures Act*, who so generously shared stories reflecting tragedy, determination, resilience and hope.

Our thanks, as well, to the eight members of the advisory committee for their knowledgeable advice, which greatly enriched our texts. We owe a sincere debt of gratitude to Magali Deleuze, Karl Hele, Lubomyr Luciuk, Laura Madokoro, Andrew Parnaby, Roberto Perin, Paul-Étienne Rainville and May Telmissany.

We would also like to express our gratitude toward the organizations and individuals who agreed to loan us objects and images from their collections, including Lillian Michiko Blakey, Ryan Boyko, Sandra Corbo, Mary Murakami Kitagawa, Marsha Forchuk Skrypuch, Norman Takeuchi, the Vocisano family, the Archives de la Ville de Montréal, the Assemblée nationale du Québec, the Canadian First World War Internment Recognition Fund, the Confederation Centre Art Gallery, the Canadian War Museum, the Musée de la police de Montréal, Pointe-à-Callière –

Montréal Archaeology and History Complex, the Nikkei National Museum, the Senate of Canada, the Sûreté du Québec, the Jehova's Witnesses and the Thomas Fisher Rare Book Library at the University of Toronto.

We want to highlight the valuable support provided by many colleagues at the Canadian Museum of History and the Canadian War Museum: Maggie Arbour, Nancy Bacon, Stacey Barker, Michelle Baxter, Andrew Burtch, Emily Compton, Tim Cook, Dave Deevey, Eric Fernberg, Anneh Fletcher, Amanda Gould, Vincent Lafond, Anne Macdonnell, Meredith MacLean, Peter MacLeod, Jeff Noakes, Christine Quinn, Kirby Sayant, Erin Wilson and Jimmy Youssef. Pascal Scallon-

Chouinard and Lee Wyndham deserve our special gratitude for their excellent work in the production of this souvenir catalogue.

We also received invaluable support from a number of external partners. Particular thanks are due to researchers Frédérique Bédard Daneau, Ivan Carel, Melissa Davidson and Joyce Pillarella, as well as cartographer François Goulet and graphic designer Sylvain Toulouse (Design Par Judith Portier inc.).

Photo Credits

p. 4-5   Photo: Michel Gravel, *La Presse*, Bibliothèque et Archives nationales du Québec, 82812 1970-10-16_p1_d

p. 7   Gift of Maurice Poggi, CWM 20020203-007

p. 9   CWM 19900029-010

p. 10-11   Matteo Omied / Alarmy Stock Photo

p. 13   Archives of Parliament

p. 15   Toronto Public Library

p. 17   CWM 19720121-086

p. 18-19   Glenbow Archives, NA-1870-6

p. 21   (left) Archives of Ontario, C 233-2-7-0-310

p. 21   (right) Archives of Ontario, C 233-2-7-0-309

p. 22-23   Map: Canadian War Museum

p. 24-25   Glenbow Archives, NC-54-4336

p. 26-27   Humphrey Album, p. 22, CMH IMG2021-0094-0008-Dm

p. 29   Gift of Lubomyr Luciuk, CMH 2017.7.4

p. 31   Loans of the Canadian First World War Internment Recognition Fund, CMH, MCH IMG2021-0130-0004-Dm and IMG2021-0130-0006-Dm

p. 32-33   Loan of Ryan Boyko, CMH IMG2021-0130-0007-Dm

p. 35   Courtesy of Marsha Forchuk Skrypuch

p. 36-37   Loans of the Canadian First World War Internment Recognition Fund, L4917.2

p. 38-39   Library and Archives Canada, PA-170620

p. 40-41   Library and Archives Canada, PA-170623

p. 43   Courtesy of the Jehovah's Witnesses

p. 44-45   Glenbow Archives, NA-5051-133

p. 46   Archives of the *Toronto Star* / Getty Images

p. 47   CWM 19920166-169

p. 48   CWM 20010129-0202

p. 49   Library and Archives Canada, 1983-30-761

p. 50   Japanese Canadien Cultural Centre, 2001.3.59

p. 51   *The Globe and Mail*, July 17, 1942, p. 3, Archives of *The Globe and Mail*

p. 53   Archives of Ontario, F 4449-1-16

p. 55   (top) CWM 20070070-026

p. 55   (bottom) CWM 20070070-021

p. 56-57   Library and Archives Canada, PA-188742

p. 58   CWM 20020203-016

p. 59   Gift of Maurice Poggi CWM 20020203-001

p. 60   Gift of Maurice Poggi, CWM 20020203-008

p. 61   Courtesy of Sandra Corbo

p. 63   Courtesy of Mary Murakami Kitagawa

p. 64-65   Loan from Mary Murakami Kitagawa, CMH IMG2021-0130-0003-Dm

p. 66-67   Tak Toyota, Library and Archives Canada, C-047398

p. 68   Courtesy of the Takeuchi family

p. 69   Gift from Norman Takeuchi,
            CWM 20140167-005

p. 70-71   Print screen of *Ipperwash Land
            Expropration: Hell of a Deal, The Fift Estate*,
            CBC, 1989

p. 72   Archives de la Ville de Montréal,
            CA M001 P146-1-2-D16-P001

p. 73   Pointe-à-Callière, Montréal Archaeology
            and History Complex 2010.71.004

p. 74   Bibliothèque et Archives nationales du
            Québec, DIS-45/05856

p. 75   Archives – Ville de Mont-Royal

p. 76-77   Photo: Duncan Cameron, Library and
            Archives Canada, 1970-015 NPC,
            e010858586-v8

p. 79   Canadian Museum of History, Archives,
            Fonds André-Duchesne, 2018-H0011.1

p. 81   MCH 2014.43.1

p. 83   Photo: Michel Gravel, *La Presse*,
            Bibliothèque et Archives nationales du
            Québec, 82812 1970-10-16_p1_d

p. 85   Associated Press, 701018012

p. 87   Gift of Tom Halley, MCG 19812910-003

p. 88-89   Associated Press, 235840504795

p. 91   Canadian Museum of History, Rare books,
            Alain-Lavigne Collection, LA 418 Q4 Q37,
            CMH IMG2021-0102-0001-Dm

p. 93   Sûreté du Québec, Photothèque,
            2008_1091

p. 94-95   Photo: Gabor Szilasi, Bibliothèque
            et Archives nationales du Québec,
            Vieux-Montréal, Fonds du ministère de la
            Culture et des Communications,
            E6, S7, SS1, 690606-3

p. 96-97   Photo: Paul Henri Talbot, Archives *La Presse*

p. 98   Photo: Jean Goupil, Bibliothèque et
            Archives nationales du Québec,
            Vieux-Montréal, fonds *La Presse*,
            P833, S2, D3923

p. 99   *Winnipeg Tribune*, Feburary 11, 1971, p. 9,
            University of Manitoba Archives and Special
            Collections

p. 100-101 © Ronald Labelle

p. 103   Canadian Heritage

p. 105   Senate of Canada,
            COM_PHO-Billc77_2021-08-11_DSC_0579

p. 106-107 Nikkei National Museum, Gordon King
            Collection, 2010-32-57

p. 109   Commissioned by
            the Unkrainian Canadian Civil Rights
            Association

p. 111   Photo: Geoff Robins, Canadian Press

p. 112-113 Photo: Serge Gouin, Royal Canadian
            Mounted Police, RCMP-SG-2018-0918-040

p. 115   Wikimedia Commons, CC BY-SA 4.0,
            Guerinf

A Message From the Canadian First World War Internment Recognition Fund

The Canadian First World War Internment Recognition Fund is pleased to support the exhibition, **Lost Liberties – The *War Measures Act.***

This exhibition will ensure that visitors to the Canadian Museum of History will learn of the effects of the *War Measures Act* and its crippling legacy, more than 100 years after it was first implemented. Congratulations to the Canadian Museum of History for telling this story, which focuses on some of the dark chapters of our Canadian history. We are hopeful that through education, this infringement on Canadian civil liberties will never happen again.

On November 25, 2005, M.P. Inky Mark's private member's Bill C-331, *Internment of Persons of Ukrainian Origin Recognition Act*, received royal assent. On May 9, 2008, following negotiations with the Ukrainian Canadian Civil Liberties Association, the Ukrainian Canadian Congress and the Ukrainian Canadian Foundation of Taras Shevchenko, the Government of Canada established the Canadian First World War Internment Recognition Fund. The Fund supports commemorative and educational initiatives that recall what happened to Ukrainians and other Europeans during Canada's first national internment operations of 1914–1920.

Borys Sirskyj
Chair
Canadian First World War Internment Recognition Fund